The Libertarian Utopia

Free Markets and Dynamic Competition

Niko Camacho

Contents

1 Introduction to Liberty

Liberty, at its core, is the right to self-determination. It's the freedom to chart your own course, to make your own choices, unburdened by undue coercion. This isn't simply about the absence of physical restraints; it's about possessing the autonomy to pursue your ambitions and live your life according to your own values, provided, of course, those pursuits don't infringe upon the equal rights of others. This fundamental freedom underpins all aspects of a thriving society, from the smallest personal decisions to the broadest economic interactions. It's the bedrock upon which we build a truly flourishing civilization, one where individuals are empowered to reach their full potential.

The assertion that liberty fosters prosperity isn't a mere conjecture; it's supported by centuries of observation and a substantial body of economic theory. When individuals are free to pursue their own economic interests, they're incentivized to innovate, to work harder, and to produce goods and services that meet the demands of a diverse marketplace. This dynamism, this constant striving for improvement, is the engine of economic growth. It's not altruism alone that drives this progress but the inherent self-interest that fuels human ambition within a system that rewards creativity and effort. The pursuit of personal gain, channeled through free markets, becomes a powerful force for societal advancement. Consider the countless innovations that have improved lives across the globe – all born from the creative energy unleashed by the pursuit of individual freedom.

Protecting individual liberty isn't simply a matter of abstract principles; it's also about safeguarding property rights. Ownership of property – whether it's land, tools, or intellectual creations – is inextricably linked to personal freedom. Without secure property rights, individuals are vulnerable to arbitrary seizure and dispossession, undermining their ability to plan for the future, invest in their own betterment, and participate fully in the economic system. This fundamental right is not merely a privilege bestowed by government; it's a prerequisite for individual autonomy and economic empowerment. It's the essential framework within which innovation flourishes and a free society thrives.

However, the concept of liberty isn't without its complexities. There are those who interpret liberty solely through a negative lens, focusing on the absence of government constraint. They might view any regulation or intervention as an infringement upon personal freedom. But a more nuanced perspective recognizes that true liberty requires not just freedom from government but also freedom to act within a framework of mutual respect and responsibility. A society committed to liberty must also ensure fairness and prevent the exploitation of others – a delicate balance that must be navigated carefully. This is not about imposing rigid controls but about establishing a just framework where everyone can exercise their rights without harming or unfairly disadvantaging their neighbors.

The argument for a free society, for a society built upon the foundations of liberty, rests not on utopian idealism but on a pragmatic understanding of human nature and the workings of the economy. It acknowledges that individuals are driven by self-interest, but it also recognizes that competition – when properly regulated – channels this self-interest in a way that creates widespread benefits. A free market, where individuals and businesses can freely enter and exit the marketplace, fosters innovation, improves efficiency, and ultimately leads to greater prosperity for all. It's a system that encourages cooperation, even while competition fuels the innovative drive of individuals striving for success. This is far from a zero-sum game; cooperation and competition are symbiotic forces that propel society forward.

The pursuit of liberty isn't a static goal; it's an ongoing process requiring constant vigilance and adaptation. As our society evolves, so too must our understanding of what constitutes true liberty and how best to protect it. This isn't a simple, one-size-fits-all formula; it involves a continual process of refining our values, institutions, and policies to better ensure that everyone has the opportunity to exercise their fundamental rights. We must be ever mindful of the potential threats to liberty—from government overreach to the erosion of individual rights—and we must remain vigilant in our commitment to preserving the freedoms upon which a just and prosperous society depends.

1.1 Defining Freedom

Freedom isn't merely the absence of physical restraints; it's a multifaceted concept encompassing individual autonomy, self-ownership, and the right to pursue one's chosen path, unburdened by undue coercion. This isn't a boundless license to harm others; instead, it's a framework that balances individual liberty with the necessity of protecting others from harm. Think of it as a carefully calibrated balance, where personal freedom thrives within a structure of mutual respect and responsibility.

Consider the implications of owning your own labor. This foundational aspect of freedom means you control your time, skills, and efforts. You determine how you utilize these assets, choosing your profession, your work hours, and your entrepreneurial ventures. This fundamental right underpins the entire free market system, providing the impetus for individual initiative and innovation. It's the bedrock upon which economic prosperity is built.

However, true freedom extends beyond the economic realm. It encompasses the freedom of thought, speech, and religion—the ability to express your beliefs without fear of reprisal, to question authority, and to engage in open dialogue. It's about the right to assemble peacefully, to associate with whomever you choose, and to form communities based on shared interests and values. These freedoms are not merely abstract ideals; they are essential elements of a vibrant and thriving society. They allow for diverse perspectives, fostering innovation and progress.

The pursuit of happiness, often overlooked in discussions of freedom, is inextricably linked to our ability to make our own choices. It's the freedom to shape our lives according to our values and aspirations, to pursue our passions, and to build a life that is meaningful to us. This is not to say that life will always be easy, or that everyone will achieve their dreams, but that the pursuit of happiness is an inherent right, protected by the principles of liberty.

Protecting individual freedoms necessitates a clear understanding of their boundaries. While we celebrate the right to self-expression, this right does not extend to infringing upon the rights of others. Freedom doesn't mean license to cause harm or to violate the rights of others, be it physical harm, theft, or fraud. A just society establishes clear rules and regulations to maintain order and protect individuals from violence and exploitation. The line is drawn not to stifle freedom, but to safeguard its essence.

The concept of property rights is central to the libertarian vision of freedom. Ownership of property – be it land, tools, or intellectual creations – provides individuals with security and control over their assets. It incentivizes investment, innovation, and productive activity, forming the engine of economic growth within a free market. Protecting these rights is not simply about safeguarding possessions; it is about upholding the fundamental right to the fruits of one's labor.

Furthermore, the freedom of contract, a cornerstone of a free society, allows individuals to voluntarily engage in economic exchange and cooperation. It empowers individuals to engage in mutual agreements, fostering trust and cooperation, which is vital for commerce and social cohesion. The absence of coercive government intervention in these transactions helps ensures the efficient allocation of resources within the market. This freedom to enter and exit contracts freely is a crucial mechanism for the natural development of the economy.

Negative freedom, characterized by the absence of external

constraints, is frequently confused with its counterpart, positive freedom. Negative freedom is the freedom from interference, from unjust laws, and from physical coercion. Positive freedom, on the other hand, focuses on the ability to act, to achieve one's potential, and to pursue one's goals. Both aspects are essential, working in tandem to create a society where individuals are both protected from oppression and empowered to achieve their aspirations. One cannot exist without the other to achieve genuine personal liberty.

A free society requires a responsible citizenry. Individuals must exercise their freedoms responsibly, understanding that their actions have consequences, both for themselves and for others. It's not simply about being free to do as one pleases, but about understanding the balance between individual liberty and social responsibility, to act in a way that does not hinder the freedom of others. Such balance is vital for the sustainability of a truly free society.

Ultimately, defining freedom is an ongoing process of reflection and discussion. It's a concept that evolves as societies grapple with new challenges and opportunities. Yet, the fundamental principles of individual autonomy, self-ownership, and the protection of individual rights remain at the heart of any true understanding of freedom. It's not a static concept, but a dynamic process that continually adapts to the evolving needs of society. The pursuit of a free society requires constant vigilance, a commitment to individual liberty, and a willingness to engage in open and respectful dialogue about its meaning and implications. This understanding is crucial to the development of a thriving society based on true freedom.

1.2 The Case for Liberty

Liberty isn't merely the absence of constraints; it's the vibrant presence of opportunity, a fertile ground where individual potential blossoms. It's the right to chart your own course, to pursue your dreams, unburdened by unnecessary governmental interference. This isn't some abstract ideal; it's the bedrock upon which a thriving society is built. Consider the countless innovations, the breathtaking advancements in technology, the sheer abundance of goods and services—all born from the fertile soil of individual liberty and free exchange. This isn't a naive belief in a perfect system, but a pragmatic understanding of human nature and the inherent power of individual agency. Restrict that agency, and you stifle progress, creativity, and ultimately, human flourishing.

The inherent dignity of each individual necessitates the protection of their rights. These are not privileges granted by the state, but fundamental entitlements inherent to being human. Among these rights, property rights stand as paramount, forming the foundation for individual autonomy and economic prosperity. Ownership fosters responsibility, encouraging careful stewardship of resources and stimulating innovation. Secure property rights fuel investment, driving economic growth and creating a wealth that benefits society as a whole. Imagine a world where individuals fear the arbitrary seizure of their property—innovation would plummet, investment would dry up, and the overall standard of living would suffer considerably. This isn't simply conjecture; historical examples abound demonstrating the inextricable link between secure property rights and economic progress.

A common critique of liberty focuses on the potential for inequality. The argument often centers on the idea that a completely free market inevitably creates vast disparities in wealth. However, this overlooks the dynamic nature of free markets and their capacity for upward mobility. While inequalities might exist, they are often the result of individual choices, differences in skill, effort, and risk-taking. A truly free market isn't static; it's constantly evolving, driven by innovation and competition, creating opportunities for individuals from all backgrounds to improve their circumstances. Moreover, a system that prioritizes individual liberty doesn't preclude voluntary efforts to address social inequality. Philanthropy, charity, and private initiatives can play a crucial role in mitigating disparities and providing assistance to those in need. These efforts, driven by individual compassion and voluntary action, are far more likely to be effective and sustainable than government-mandated programs.

Furthermore, the claim that unchecked liberty leads to environmental destruction ignores the powerful incentives for environmental stewardship inherent in a free market. When individuals own property, they have a vested interest in preserving its value, including its environmental integrity. The market provides solutions through incentivizing sustainable practices, fostering innovation in clean technologies, and rewarding businesses that prioritize environmental responsibility. Contrast this with a centrally planned economy where environmental damage is often rampant due to a lack of accountability and the absence of market-based incentives. By contrast, private property rights, coupled with robust market mechanisms, offer a far more effective and sustainable solution.

Ultimately, the case for liberty rests on its ability to unleash human potential, fostering innovation, prosperity, and a dynamic society responsive to individual needs. It's not about a lack of regulation; it's about limiting government intervention to its most essential functions—protecting individual rights, enforcing contracts, and providing for national defense. Beyond this, the market, guided by the invisible hand of competition and individual choice, is far better equipped to allocate resources, drive innovation, and ultimately create a more prosperous and just society. It is a system that not only empowers individuals but also harnesses the collective wisdom of millions, leading to a greater good than any centrally planned system could hope to achieve. Liberty, therefore, isn't just a political ideal; it's a practical pathway to a more flourishing and equitable world. Its principles must remain central to our economic and social vision for a brighter future.

2 Free Market Fundamentals

Understanding supply and demand is fundamental. It's the engine driving resource allocation in a free market. Imagine a bustling farmer's market – overflowing with vibrant produce, each stall a testament to the interaction of supply and demand. A plentiful harvest leads to lower prices, attracting more buyers. Conversely, a poor yield results in higher prices, perhaps even rationing. This dynamic, constantly adjusting, ensures resources are used efficiently, a critical component of a thriving economy. It's not just about the price of apples; it's about the intricate dance between producers and consumers, their choices shaping the market itself. This understanding is crucial for anyone navigating the complexities of a free market system.

Price signals, often overlooked, are the silent messengers of the market. They're the vital information channels informing producers about consumer preferences and resource scarcity.

High prices scream, "Consumers want more, and resources are tight!" This alerts producers to increase production, invest in innovation, or explore alternative resources. Conversely, low prices whisper, "Consumers aren't interested enough to justify this much production." This signals producers to reduce output, perhaps shifting their focus to more profitable goods. Essentially, prices reflect the relative value consumers place on a good or service. Ignoring these vital signals leads to misallocation of resources and economic inefficiency. Therefore, understanding how price signals work is essential for efficient market functioning.

Competition is more than just rival businesses vying for customers; it's the lifeblood of a free market. It pushes innovation, forcing businesses to constantly improve their products and services to stay ahead. Consider the relentless advancement of technology, driven by companies competing for market share. Think about the constant evolution of smartphones, a testament to the innovative power of competition. Without this pressure, innovation stagnates, and consumers suffer. This dynamic competition leads not only to better products but also to fairer prices and greater efficiency. Furthermore, it fosters a climate of entrepreneurship, allowing new businesses to challenge established players and create new markets. Competition is the cornerstone of a dynamic and responsive economy, ensuring that resources are used effectively and that con-

sumer needs are met. In a truly free market, the consumer reigns supreme, exercising their power through choices in the marketplace. This consumer sovereignty is another essential aspect of a healthy competitive environment.
The free market isn't a perfect utopia, devoid of issues. However, it's a remarkably self-correcting system, naturally inclined towards efficiency. Consider the sheer scale of global trade, a complex network of billions of individual transactions, largely self-regulating. While some interventions might seem necessary, history repeatedly shows that excessive government intervention often creates more problems than it solves, distorting markets and hindering their inherent efficiency. Therefore, it's crucial to adopt a discerning approach, understanding that the free market, with its flaws, usually offers the best path towards prosperity and growth. This system, while imperfect, proves consistently more efficient than centrally planned economies. Maintaining faith in its natural correcting mechanisms often yields the best outcomes.
Even within the framework of a free market, challenges exist. One significant hurdle is the issue of information asymmetry. This refers to situations where one party in a transaction has significantly more information than the other, leading to potentially unfair outcomes. Imagine buying a used car – the seller likely knows more about its history and mechanical condition than the buyer. This imbalance can create inefficiencies

and even market failures. However, solutions exist, such as increased transparency and independent verification services. These attempts to level the playing field highlight the importance of addressing such imbalances without compromising the fundamental principles of the free market. The goal is to promote fairness while preserving the strengths of competitive dynamics.

2.1 Supply and Demand

Understanding the interplay of supply and demand is fundamental to grasping the dynamism of a free market. Imagine a bustling marketplace, overflowing with vendors offering a variety of goods. The quantity of each item available—the supply—is determined by producers' willingness and ability to bring goods to market at different prices. Simultaneously, consumers, with their varying needs and desires, signal their demand through their willingness to pay for those goods at different prices. This constant push and pull, this negotiation between what's available and what's wanted, dictates the price.

The simplest illustration involves a single commodity, say, apples. If the harvest is bountiful, leading to a surplus of apples, the supply increases. All else equal, this abundance pushes the price down; consumers can purchase apples at a lower cost. Conversely, if a severe frost decimates the apple crop, diminishing the supply, prices are likely to rise, reflecting the scarcity. This basic principle governs not just apples but every conceivable good and service in a free market.

But the reality is far more complex. Supply isn't a static number; it shifts based on factors like production costs, technology, and even the availability of substitute goods. For example, a technological breakthrough that streamlines apple production would increase the supply, again putting downward pressure on prices. Or perhaps the price of oranges, a substitute for apples, drops sharply, diverting consumer demand. Therefore, understanding supply necessitates considering these dynamic influences and their impact on availability.

Demand, likewise, isn't fixed. It responds to factors such as consumer income, preferences, and even expectations of future prices. A rise in consumer income, for example, could lead to an increase in the demand for apples, driving up the price. If a health report highlights the benefits of apples, this would also lead to a surge in demand. Conversely, a widespread belief that apple prices will soon fall might cause consumers to postpone their purchases, thus lowering demand in the short term.

The beauty of a free market lies in the invisible hand that guides these forces. Prices act as signals, communicating information between producers and consumers. High prices signal scarcity, prompting producers to increase supply and encouraging consumers to seek alternatives or reduce their consumption. Conversely, low prices signal abundance, encouraging consumption while potentially discouraging further production until the equilibrium is restored.

However, it is crucial to acknowledge the imperfections of the system. Information asymmetry, for instance, can lead to distortions. A lack of complete information on either side—suppliers may underestimate demand or consumers might be unaware of better deals—prevents the true supply-demand equilibrium from being efficiently reached. Similarly, government intervention, even well-intentioned, can disrupt the natural flow of the market by artificially influencing prices or restricting supply. These issues will be explored in detail in later chapters.

Ultimately, the free interplay of supply and demand underpins the dynamism and efficiency of a competitive market. It's a continuous process of adjustment, a delicate dance between producers and consumers, each responding to the signals sent by prices. By understanding this fundamental mechanism, we can better appreciate the benefits of a free market system. This model provides an efficient resource allocation, incentivizes innovation, and ultimately contributes to a more prosperous society, while recognizing the limitations and the need for a proper balance between the free market and limited government intervention.

2.2 Price Signals

Prices, in a free market, aren't arbitrary numbers slapped onto goods; they're dynamic signals, constantly shifting to reflect the intricate dance of supply and demand. Imagine a farmer bringing his harvest to market. If the demand for apples is high – perhaps it's apple pie season – the price will climb. This isn't greed; it's simply a reflection of scarcity. Higher prices incentivize the farmer to plant more apple trees next year, perhaps even inspiring others to join the apple-growing business. Conversely, if apples are abundant, the price drops, potentially signaling the farmer to plant fewer trees or even switch to a different crop entirely. This continuous feedback loop, driven by price signals, ensures resources flow to where they are most valued.

This seemingly simple mechanism underpins the incredible efficiency of free markets. It's not a centrally planned system where a bureaucrat dictates production and distribution; instead, it's a decentralized, self-regulating system where millions of individual decisions, guided by price signals, collectively determine what's produced, how much is produced, and who gets it. Prices act as the language of the market, communicating vital information to producers and consumers alike. A rise in the price of gasoline, for instance, doesn't just mean filling your tank will cost more; it signals a shortage, potentially encouraging consumers to conserve fuel and prompting energy companies to invest in exploration and alternative energy sources. The opposite is equally true: a drop in price can lead to increased consumption and possibly reduced investment.

Understanding price signals is crucial for anyone participating in a free market, whether as a consumer or a producer. For consumers, it means recognizing that higher prices often reflect a combination of increased demand or higher production costs, not necessarily exploitation. It also encourages smart shopping habits \item searching for alternatives or delaying purchases when prices are high. For producers, price signals are indispensable for making informed decisions about production. They provide vital feedback on consumer preferences, helping businesses to allocate resources effectively and adapt to changing market conditions. Ignoring these signals can lead to disastrous consequences, such as overproduction of unwanted goods or shortages of in-demand products.

Think about a new technology. If the initial price is high – reflecting the cost of research, development, and limited supply – only early adopters might afford it. As technology improves and production increases, prices tend to fall, making it accessible to a wider range of consumers. This dynamic isn't merely about affordability; it's a testament to the market's inherent drive toward efficiency. The initial high price encourages innovation, attracting investment and competition, which eventually lowers prices and benefits everyone. This principle extends far beyond technology. Consider the historical trend of decreasing prices in nearly all consumer goods, a direct result of competitive innovation fueled by those very price signals.

But the power of price signals isn't without its limitations. Distortions can arise from government intervention, such as price controls or subsidies. Price ceilings, for example, artificially limit how high a price can go, creating shortages and fostering black markets. Subsidies, on the other hand, artificially lower prices, potentially leading to overproduction and misallocation of resources. These interventions disrupt the natural flow of information inherent in price signals, leading to inefficiencies and unintended consequences. A truly free market allows prices to fluctuate freely, providing the most accurate reflection of supply and demand, thus optimally guiding resource allocation and ensuring the most efficient and equitable distribution of goods and services. In essence, allowing the market to function according to the signals of pricing is essential for prosperity and growth. The clear, undistorted communication of this information is imperative to economic health and wellbeing. Therefore, minimizing interference to allow the market's natural mechanisms to thrive is paramount.

2.3 Competition's Role

Competition isn't merely a feature of a free market; it's the very lifeblood. Without it, the dynamism that propels innovation, efficiency, and economic growth stagnates. Imagine a world with only one provider of, say, internet service. The lack of alternatives would likely lead to higher prices, poorer service, and a stifled innovation, a stark contrast to the competitive landscape we experience today. This is why understanding competition's role is paramount to grasping the true potential of a free market.

Consider the smartphone market. Years ago, options were limited and prices were high. The emergence of numerous competitors, each vying for market share through innovation and competitive pricing, fundamentally changed the industry. Today, we have a vast array of choices, sophisticated technology, and affordable prices—a direct result of the competitive pressure. This illustrates how competition directly benefits the consumer.

But the advantages extend beyond affordability. Competition fosters innovation. Companies constantly strive to offer superior products or services to gain a competitive edge. This drive fuels the development of new technologies, improved designs, and enhanced features. Think of the relentless improvement in computing power, screen resolution, and camera technology in smartphones. This continuous improvement is a direct consequence of competition driving companies to outdo one another.

Furthermore, competition ensures efficiency. Businesses under competitive pressure are incentivized to minimize costs and maximize productivity. Wasteful practices are quickly eliminated as companies strive to operate leanly and efficiently to compete effectively. This efficiency translates into lower prices for consumers and improved allocation of resources throughout the economy. It's a constant striving for optimization, a perpetual improvement cycle driven by the competitive environment.

However, the competitive landscape isn't always perfect. Monopolies and oligopolies, where a small number of firms dominate the market, can stifle competition and lead to reduced innovation, higher prices, and decreased consumer choice. Understanding these potential pitfalls and implementing appropriate safeguards—while still upholding libertarian principles—is crucial. This is not to advocate for government intervention but rather for a keen awareness of the factors that can undermine a truly competitive marketplace.

Competition isn't just about lower prices, although that's a significant benefit. It's also about providing consumers with choices. In a competitive market, businesses have to offer something unique or better to attract customers. This results in a broader range of products and services tailored to diverse needs and preferences. The abundance of choice itself improves consumer welfare significantly, beyond merely lower pricing.

The power of competition extends beyond the immediate marketplace. It's a driving force for economic growth. By fostering innovation, efficiency, and consumer choice, competition creates a virtuous cycle of progress. It incentivizes investment, expands employment opportunities, and ultimately improves overall standards of living. Economic growth isn't a passive event but rather the outcome of this dynamic competitive environment. The prosperity we enjoy today is fundamentally linked to its competitive nature.

However, it is important to acknowledge that some markets may naturally lend themselves to fewer competitors. This is not necessarily a sign of market failure, but rather a reflection of the specific characteristics of the industry. The challenge lies in ensuring that these naturally occurring scenarios do not lead to exploitative practices or the stifling of innovation. Regulation should remain focused on preventing anti-competitive behavior rather than artificially creating competition where it does not organically emerge.

The role of competition in a libertarian utopia is pivotal. It's not just a mechanism for economic efficiency; it's a fundamental driver of progress, innovation, and consumer well-being.

By understanding its dynamics and potential pitfalls, we can better cultivate a vibrant and flourishing free market that maximizes liberty and prosperity for all. Protecting and nurturing a competitive landscape is essential for realizing the full potential of a free society. The focus should remain on empowering individuals, protecting their rights, and ensuring the conditions necessary for vigorous competition to thrive. This dynamic interplay between freedom and competition underpins the very essence of a libertarian ideal. It is not merely a theoretical construct, but a practical engine for human advancement. Without competition, the promise of a free market remains unrealized. Its vital role demands constant vigilance and a steadfast commitment to the principles of liberty.

3 The Power of Competition

Competition, the lifeblood of a free market, isn't merely a theoretical concept; it's a dynamic force shaping our daily lives. It's the reason we have access to a staggering array of goods and services, constantly improving in quality and decreasing in price. This constant striving for excellence, fueled by the desire to win customers, drives innovation and efficiency in ways that centralized planning simply cannot match.

Consider the smartphone market. Years ago, a basic cell phone was a luxury. Today, smartphones boast incredible processing power, high-resolution cameras, and access to a universe of information, all at prices significantly lower than their predecessors. This dramatic improvement, this rapid advancement, is a direct result of fierce competition between companies battling for market share. Each vying for the attention of consumers, pushing the boundaries of technology and design. This isn't just about profit maximization; it's about delivering value to consumers, who are, ultimately, the ultimate arbiters.

Consumer sovereignty, a cornerstone of the free market, empowers individuals. We are not passive recipients of goods and services dictated by a central authority. Instead, we actively shape the market through our purchasing decisions. Our choices influence what products are developed, how they're designed, and ultimately, their prices. This dynamic feedback loop ensures that businesses respond to our wants and needs, driving constant adaptation and improvement. Imagine a world where you had only one choice for your phone, or your car, or your groceries – a stark contrast to the vibrant and diverse marketplace we enjoy today.

The efficiency gains derived from competition are profound and far-reaching. In competitive markets, businesses are constantly seeking ways to optimize their processes, reduce costs, and increase productivity. Waste is minimized, resources are utilized effectively, and innovation is fostered. This inherent drive for efficiency isn't merely beneficial to businesses; it translates into lower prices and higher-quality goods for consumers. The relentless pursuit of greater efficiency isn't merely a means to an end; it's a self-perpetuating cycle that benefits the entire economy.

Economic growth, often cited as a primary indicator of a healthy economy, is intrinsically linked to competition. Innovation, a direct consequence of competitive pressure, leads to new products, new services, and new industries. This expansion of the economic pie creates new jobs, increases overall wealth, and raises living standards. This isn't just about abstract economic theories; it's about the tangible improvements in our lives, from better healthcare to more efficient transportation, all born from the crucible of competition. History shows a clear correlation: vibrant, competitive markets are engines of economic progress.

Reduced prices, a direct and tangible benefit of competition, directly improve the well-being of consumers. When multiple businesses compete for the same customer, they are forced to lower their prices to remain competitive. This price competition ensures that consumers receive the most value for their money, enhancing their purchasing power and overall standard of living. This is not a zero-sum game; it's a win-win situation where both businesses and consumers benefit from the dynamics of the market. The constant pressure to reduce costs and offer competitive pricing drives the market toward greater efficiency and consumer satisfaction. Lower prices mean more choices, greater accessibility, and a higher standard of living for everyone. The power of competition is, ultimately, the power of choice.

The benefits of competition extend far beyond mere economic indicators. It fosters innovation, empowers consumers, enhances efficiency, fuels economic growth, and reduces prices.

Competition is not just a feature of a free market; it is the very engine that drives its success. It's a dynamic, ever-evolving process that constantly adapts to the changing needs and preferences of consumers, ensuring a marketplace that is responsive, efficient, and ultimately beneficial for all participants.

3.1 Innovation's Engine

Competition isn't merely a force; it's the very engine driving innovation. Think of the relentless pursuit of a better mousetrap, a more efficient process, a more desirable product. This isn't altruism; it's the self-interest of entrepreneurs striving for market dominance, a battle waged not with swords and shields, but with ingenuity and efficiency. The constant pressure to outperform rivals forces companies to push boundaries, explore uncharted territories, and relentlessly refine their offerings. This dynamic competition isn't just about profit maximization; it's about satisfying consumer desires in novel and compelling ways.

Consider the history of computing. From bulky room-sized mainframes to sleek smartphones capable of unimaginable processing power, the journey reflects this relentless innovation. Each incremental improvement, each breakthrough, was fueled by the competition among companies vying for market share. This wasn't a coordinated effort; it was a chaotic dance of individual ambition, leading to an extraordinary collective advancement. We see this pattern repeated across countless industries – automobiles, pharmaceuticals, telecommunications – each evolving at an accelerated pace due to this same powerful dynamic.

The absence of competition, conversely, leads to stagnation. Monopolies, by their very nature, lack the incentive for constant improvement. With no fear of losing market share, there's little impetus to innovate, to invest in research and development, or to cater to the evolving needs of consumers. The result is often inferior products, higher prices, and ultimately, a less dynamic economy. This isn't just theoretical; numerous historical examples demonstrate the stifling effect of monopolies on progress.

But it's not only about large corporations; the spirit of competition thrives even at a smaller scale. Entrepreneurs launching startups often face daunting challenges, yet they persist, driven by the desire to create something new, something better. This desire for success isn't simply a matter of wealth accumulation; it's also about the intrinsic satisfaction of creating something valuable, of providing a solution to a problem, of contributing to the marketplace with one's unique skills and vision. This personal drive, multiplied across a free market, creates a powerful force for innovation.

This constant push for improvement isn't limited to tangible products. It extends to services, processes, and even business models. Consider the rise of e-commerce, disrupting traditional retail through innovative platforms and approaches to customer engagement. The very competitive nature of online marketplaces has compelled companies to constantly refine their offerings, leading to a continuous cycle of improvement. This process, while often disruptive, ultimately benefits consumers through increased choice, lower prices, and more convenient services.

Moreover, the freedom to compete fosters a vibrant ecosystem of creativity. Entrepreneurs and innovators aren't constrained by government regulations or bureaucratic hurdles; instead, they are free to experiment, to fail, and to learn from their mistakes. This experimentation, this iterative process of trial and error, is essential to the innovation process. The willingness to take risks, to invest in unproven ideas, is a hallmark of a dynamic, competitive market.

Of course, competition isn't always perfect. It can lead to unintended consequences, such as cutthroat pricing strategies or unethical practices. But these issues are often self-correcting, as consumers gravitate towards companies that provide high-quality products and services at fair prices. Furthermore, the robust marketplace is a self-regulating system. Failures, while sometimes painful, serve as a vital component of the constant cycle of improvement. The market is not static; it's a dynamic and adaptive system capable of adjusting and evolving.

Furthermore, it's crucial to remember that competition doesn't necessitate cutthroat behavior or unethical practices. Ethical competition thrives on fair play, transparency, and a commitment to providing genuine value to consumers. A level playing field, where all participants adhere to a code of ethical conduct, fosters a healthy competitive environment, promoting innovation without sacrificing integrity. This ethical approach to competition creates a sustainable environment that benefits everyone involved, not only the businesses that participate but also the consumers they serve. In essence, ethical competition forms the cornerstone of sustainable economic growth and consumer satisfaction.

Therefore, understanding the engine of innovation means recognizing the fundamental role of competition in a free market. It is through the relentless pursuit of excellence, the striving to outperform rivals, that we achieve advancements that improve lives, enhance efficiency, and drive economic growth. It's a dynamic, self-correcting process that, while imperfect, offers the most robust and reliable pathway to progress. A competitive market is not merely about maximizing profits; it's about providing better solutions, creating value, and improving the world. The constant pursuit of improvement, spurred by competition, is the cornerstone of a thriving society, a society constantly pushing the boundaries of what's possible.

3.2 Consumer Sovereignty

Consumer sovereignty, at its core, represents the ultimate authority of the consumer in directing the production and distribution of goods and services. It's not just a theoretical concept; it's the driving force behind a truly dynamic and responsive market. In a free market, businesses thrive not by dictating what consumers should want, but by understanding and responding to their desires. This responsiveness ensures that resources are allocated efficiently, mirroring the actual needs and preferences of society, rather than being distorted by government intervention or the whims of powerful corporations. It's a powerful mechanism ensuring that the market serves the people, and not the other way around.

This principle directly contradicts the top-down approach of centrally planned economies where production decisions are made by a select few, often disconnected from the everyday needs of the population. Imagine a world where your choice of clothing, food, or even housing is limited by government quotas or bureaucratic decisions. This lacks the dynamism and flexibility of a free market, resulting in shortages, surpluses, and a general lack of satisfaction for the average consumer. Consumer sovereignty, on the other hand, provides a constant feedback loop, where success is directly tied to understanding and fulfilling consumer demands.

This powerful force creates a virtuous cycle of innovation and improvement. Companies constantly strive to offer better products at competitive prices, driven by the simple fact that consumers will choose the options that best suit their needs and budget. This competition is not merely about price wars; it's about enhancing quality, introducing new features, and providing a superior customer experience. Therefore, the consumer benefits not only from lower prices but also from a broader range of choices and higher quality goods, constantly pushing businesses to improve and innovate.

Let's take the example of the smartphone market. Several decades ago, cell phones were bulky, expensive, and had limited functionality. Yet, as consumer demand for smaller, more powerful, and feature-rich devices grew, companies responded with innovation, leading to the sleek and sophisticated smartphones we use today. This evolution wasn't orchestrated by government planning but was driven by the collective choices of millions of consumers, a testament to the power of consumer sovereignty.

However, this dynamic system isn't without its challenges. Factors like information asymmetry—where consumers lack complete knowledge about products or services—can impede consumer sovereignty. Similarly, externalities, such as environmental damage from production, can lead to market failures. Addressing these challenges requires finding ways to ensure consumers are well-informed and businesses internalize the costs of their actions, perhaps through labeling requirements or carbon taxes. These mechanisms aim to enhance market transparency and efficiency, without compromising the fundamental principle of consumer choice.

Moreover, consumer sovereignty isn't solely about individual choices; it's also about the collective influence of consumer preferences shaping market trends. Think about the increasing demand for sustainable and ethically produced goods. This collective preference is pushing businesses to adapt their practices, leading to the growth of eco-friendly products and a greater focus on corporate social responsibility. This shows the power of consumers, not just individually but collectively, to influence the direction of the market.

Furthermore, understanding consumer sovereignty isn't merely about accepting market outcomes passively. It requires active participation and engagement. Being an informed consumer, comparing prices, researching products, and providing feedback to businesses all contribute to shaping the marketplace and ensuring your preferences are heard. It's about using your economic power to drive positive changes in the market, from promoting sustainable businesses to demanding better quality products.

In conclusion, consumer sovereignty is not simply a desirable outcome of free markets; it's the very engine that drives their efficiency and dynamism. It represents the fundamental right of consumers to determine what goods and services are produced, effectively allocating resources based on actual need and preferences. While challenges exist, such as information asymmetry and externalities, actively participating in the market and advocating for responsible business practices ensures that the power remains firmly with the consumer. The result is a market that constantly adapts, innovates, and improves, providing a more efficient, responsive, and satisfying experience for all. This is the bedrock of a thriving free market and a key element of a truly libertarian utopia.

3.3 Efficiency Gains

Imagine a bustling marketplace, overflowing with diverse goods and services. Each vendor, driven by self-interest, strives to attract customers. This competition, seemingly cutthroat, is the engine of remarkable efficiency. It forces producers to innovate, to refine their products, and to deliver exceptional value for the price, creating a dynamic system where consumer demand guides resource allocation with remarkable precision. This isn't some theoretical ideal; it's a demonstrable truth reflected in countless examples throughout history. The relentless pursuit of profit in a free market, far from being purely selfish, inadvertently benefits society as a whole.

Consider the evolution of the personal computer. In the early days, machines were bulky, expensive, and possessed limited capabilities. But the intense competition between manufacturers spurred rapid innovation. Prices steadily decreased as technology advanced, making computers accessible to a wider population. This process wasn't planned or coordinated; it emerged organically from the competitive dynamics of a free market. Each company striving for the best product, the lowest price, ultimately created a better outcome for consumers, an outcome that a centrally planned system could never achieve with the same efficiency.

Efficiency gains aren't merely about lower prices, though that's certainly a significant benefit. It's about optimizing resource allocation. In a free market, resources flow towards their most productive uses. A manufacturer who wastes resources will eventually find themselves unable to compete with more efficient rivals. This constant pressure to eliminate waste and streamline operations leads to remarkable gains in productivity and overall efficiency across the entire economy. Think of it as a continuous process of refinement, driven by the invisible hand of the market.

This isn't to say that a free market is perfect. It's a dynamic and complex system, subject to occasional disruptions and imbalances. But these are usually self-correcting, and the market's ability to adapt and innovate far surpasses the capacity of any government bureaucracy. Government intervention, while sometimes necessary to address specific market failures, often stifles competition and hinders efficiency gains. Regulations, while intending to help, can inadvertently create barriers to entry for new businesses, reduce innovation, and ultimately lead to higher prices and lower quality products for consumers.

The efficiency gains derived from free markets extend beyond the immediate exchange of goods and services. They ripple throughout society, fostering economic growth, creating jobs, and improving the overall standard of living. This isn't simply a matter of theoretical economics; ample empirical evidence supports this claim. Studies have consistently shown a strong correlation between economic freedom and economic growth. Countries with more free markets tend to experience higher levels of prosperity and improved living standards for their citizens. The increased productivity fueled by competition translates directly into a larger and more dynamic economy.

But the benefits go beyond mere economic metrics. Efficiency gains free up resources that can be allocated towards other pursuits – arts, culture, scientific research, and countless other activities that enhance human lives. When businesses are efficient, they require fewer resources to produce the same level of output, releasing individuals to pursue their passions and enriching society in ways that are difficult to quantify but are profoundly important nonetheless. This liberation of resources isn't a side effect; it's a direct consequence of the inherent efficiency of free markets.

Furthermore, consider the individual level. In a competitive market, individuals are empowered to pursue their own goals and ambitions. Entrepreneurs are free to innovate, and consumers are free to choose the goods and services that best meet their needs. This fosters a dynamic and creative environment, driving innovation and progress. It's a system where individual initiative is rewarded and where success is driven by merit, not by political connections or government favoritism. The resulting efficiency gains are then not just economic, but social and individual as well. The freedom to pursue your own path, to innovate and compete, leads to a more vibrant and fulfilling society.

The pursuit of efficiency isn't a cold, impersonal calculation. It's a dynamic process that reflects human ingenuity and the drive to improve. It's about constant innovation, a relentless striving to do things better, faster, and more efficiently. This relentless striving, however, is not a result of some grand plan or central authority; it's the inherent nature of a competitive free market. It's the invisible hand guiding resources to their most productive uses, shaping a world where efficiency isn't merely a goal, but a constant, ongoing process of improvement. This constant improvement, constantly driven by competition, directly increases the overall efficiency of the market.

In a free market system, efficiency gains aren't just about the bottom line; they're about creating a better world for everyone. They're about empowering individuals, fostering innovation, and providing a higher quality of life for all members of society. The benefits are not limited to economic growth; they extend to social progress, cultural enrichment, and the overall well-being of humanity. This profound interconnectedness between efficiency and societal advancement is a testament to the power of free markets and the inherent human drive to improve. And as we progress, our capacity to increase efficiency only grows with the market.

3.4 Economic Growth

Economic growth isn't some abstract concept; it's the tangible improvement in our collective well-being, manifested in higher standards of living, more opportunities, and increased societal prosperity. It's not just about bigger numbers on a spreadsheet; it's about real people enjoying better lives, having access to a wider range of goods and services, and experiencing greater fulfillment. The engine driving this positive change, in a free market system, is dynamic competition.

Competition, in its purest form, isn't about cutthroat tactics or malicious intent. Instead, it's a vibrant dance of innovation and efficiency, where businesses strive to provide the best products and services at the most competitive prices to attract consumers. This continuous improvement, this relentless striving for excellence, fuels economic expansion. Businesses are constantly seeking new and better ways to produce goods and services. Consider the smartphone market: decades ago, phones were bulky and expensive; today, many people own sleek, powerful devices with advanced capabilities that cost a fraction of their predecessors. This is the power of competitive innovation in action.

This competitive pressure isn't limited to the products themselves. It extends to production methods, logistics, and even marketing strategies. Companies constantly seek ways to reduce costs without sacrificing quality, streamline their operations, and reach more consumers efficiently. This continuous efficiency drive leads to lower prices for consumers, making goods and services more accessible to a wider population. A larger market, with consumers able to purchase more, naturally contributes to economic expansion. And it's a self-reinforcing cycle: lower prices stimulate demand, which in turn encourages further innovation and efficiency improvements.

The effect extends far beyond individual transactions. Competition fosters a constant drive toward innovation, leading to the creation of new industries, new jobs, and entirely new ways of living. Think about the internet and the countless industries it has spawned—e-commerce, social media, cloud computing—all born out of competitive pressures and the desire to provide consumers with better experiences. The benefits are felt across society, creating new opportunities for entrepreneurs, fostering technological advancements, and enriching the lives of everyone who participates in the economy. Economic expansion is not just a matter of financial gains but also a testament to human ingenuity and enterprise.

Moreover, the increased productivity resulting from competition isn't limited to the private sector; it also has a substantial positive impact on government services. A thriving economy translates into a larger tax base, providing governments with more resources to fund essential public services such as education, infrastructure, and healthcare. This enhanced capacity allows for improved public services and a higher quality of life for all citizens. Conversely, a stagnant or shrinking economy restricts public resources, negatively affecting the provision of essential services. Consequently, economic growth is not just about private wealth accumulation, but also plays a vital role in promoting social welfare.

Yet, the benefits of a competitive market aren't guaranteed; their realization depends on a well-defined framework that protects and encourages competition. This means a legal system that enforces contracts, protects intellectual property, and prevents monopolies from stifling innovation. Without these safeguards, the potential for economic growth is significantly reduced. A system that allows for the fair and free exchange of goods and services, protected by impartial law, becomes a foundation for the expansion of the economy. This is why fostering fair competition is not merely a matter of economic policy but a cornerstone of creating a truly prosperous society. Ultimately, the pursuit of economic growth within a framework of free markets and dynamic competition isn't simply about accumulating wealth; it's about building a society that offers opportunities for everyone, where innovation flourishes, and where the pursuit of progress is a continuous, self-reinforcing cycle. It's about creating a more just and prosperous future for all. This requires, above all, a deep understanding of the principles of free markets and a commitment to maintaining a system that allows the forces of competition to work their magic.

3.5 Reduced Prices

Lower prices aren't merely a desirable outcome of free markets; they're a fundamental consequence of dynamic competition. This inherent pressure to reduce prices benefits consumers directly, boosting their purchasing power and improving their overall standard of living. Imagine a world where competition is stifled; prices would inevitably rise, reducing accessibility to goods and services for everyone except the wealthiest individuals. This scenario directly contradicts the ideal of a libertarian utopia.

The mechanism is straightforward. When multiple businesses vie for the same consumer dollars, they're driven to offer increasingly attractive prices. This isn't simply about slashing profit margins, it's about increasing market share. A business that undercuts its competitors, while maintaining profitability through efficiency and smart cost management, can attract a larger customer base, leading to greater overall revenue. This constant drive for improvement fuels a cycle of ever-lower prices and improved quality in a virtuous competitive loop.

But it's not just about the initial price point; it's also about the long-term impact. Businesses are constantly challenged to innovate and increase efficiency to sustain their competitive edge and keep prices down. This innovation doesn't only benefit consumers through cheaper goods but also creates new products and services, expanding the market and further increasing consumer choices. Imagine the improvements in technology, for example, a direct result of the competitive pressure to develop better and more cost-effective products.

Furthermore, reduced prices promote economic growth. Increased affordability leads to higher consumer spending. This increased demand stimulates further production, creating jobs and stimulating economic activity across the board. A society with readily accessible goods and services naturally fosters a more vibrant and prosperous economy. Consider the historical examples of periods of intense competition, often correlated with periods of significant economic expansion. These are not mere coincidences but direct causal links.

This isn't to say that lower prices are always a perfect indicator of superior goods or services. However, in a truly competitive market, consumers have the power to discern value and price discrepancies. Low prices without the benefit of quality eventually lead to businesses failing and exiting the market, leaving only those who can meet both price and quality expectations. This constant quality-price dynamic within a competitive system is the mechanism that guarantees long-term consumer benefits.

Consumers in a free market are not passive recipients; they are active participants. They wield their purchasing power, influencing the direction of the market by rewarding businesses that offer value for money and punishing those that fail to do so. This mechanism of consumer sovereignty underpins the entire process; it keeps businesses on their toes, driving innovation, efficiency, and inevitably, lower prices. It's a self-regulating system, designed to serve consumer interests.

Reduced prices are not simply a happy byproduct of free markets; they are a direct and essential feature. They reflect the dynamism and competitiveness at the heart of a libertarian economic system. They are a testament to the power of individual choice and the benefits of a system where businesses

are constantly striving to better serve c
self-correction mechanisms and the c
cycle ensure that prices consistently re
way. Furthermore, the economic gro
tem creates a positive feedback loop,
of lower prices all the more pronounc
a system built to empower consumer
Finally, the impact of reduced price
financial gain; it affects societal well-
able goods and services significantl
life for all members of society. It enal
their needs and aspirations, boosting
tentment within a society. This enha
fosters a more stable and productive
social harmony and progress. A so
duced prices for its citizens lays the
prosperity, and, consequently, impro
all involved. This is a core pillar in
sustainable and thriving community,
reduced prices far beyond monetary
pact is holistic and far-reaching, crea
economic growth and improved qual

4 Government's Proper Role

A government's role, within a truly free society, should be profoundly limited. Its primary function is the protection of individual rights—the very cornerstone upon which a flourishing free market rests. This means securing property rights, upholding contracts, and ensuring a just legal system, free from corruption and undue influence. It's about establishing the rules of the game, not playing the game itself. Think of a referee in a sporting event; their intervention is necessary to maintain fair play, but they shouldn't dictate the strategies or outcomes. Similarly, a minimal government acts as a neutral arbiter, preventing force and fraud, not dictating economic activity.

Unlike many systems where the government attempts to control or manipulate markets—deciding which industries should thrive, or picking winners and losers—a libertarian model recognizes the inherent wisdom of millions of individuals making their own economic choices. The government's interference in such a system only distorts natural price signals, hindering the very efficiency the free market is designed to generate. It's not a question of eliminating all government; rather, it's about a radical reduction in scope and scale, focusing on those essential functions that benefit everyone equally.

Consider national defense, for example. A strong military capable of deterring foreign aggression is a public good that the free market alone cannot reliably provide. The collective action problem prevents individuals from effectively coordinating their defense, leading to potential vulnerability. However, even this critical function should be subject to rigorous oversight and accountability to ensure that it doesn't become a tool of oppression or a vehicle for wasteful spending. It needs to be limited, efficient, and truly focus on its core mission—protection of the nation's borders and interests. Overreach into other areas, such as domestic surveillance or foreign policy interventions that benefit specific corporations, clearly violate the principles of limited government.

Efficient, limited government also requires transparent and accessible legal frameworks. Everyone should have equal access to justice, regardless of their wealth or social standing. Justice, in this context, isn't about providing social services or redistributing wealth; it's about enforcing contracts and resolving disputes impartially. Clear and consistently applied laws are crucial for creating a predictable and stable environment where individuals can confidently engage in economic transactions. This also necessitates an impartial and non-corrupt judiciary, free from political pressure and influence.

Beyond the core functions of protecting individual rights and providing essential public services, government involvement should be approached with extreme caution. Subsidies, regulations, and interventions aimed at "fixing" perceived market failures often create unforeseen consequences, distorting incentives and undermining the very efficiency they intend to improve. While acknowledging that the market can be prone to imperfections, the potential harm of poorly designed government interventions frequently outweighs the perceived benefits. A more hands-off approach, allowing individuals to freely respond to market signals and innovate, almost always proves more efficient and conducive to long-term economic growth.

The true measure of a limited government isn't the size of its budget, but its impact on individual liberty and economic freedom. It's about ensuring a level playing field where individuals can pursue their own interests without unnecessary restrictions, where the focus is on empowering individuals, not controlling them. This fundamental shift from a controlling, centralized authority to an enabling and protective government—a guardian of individual rights—is the key to creating a truly libertarian utopia. A government that prioritizes the protection of liberty above all else allows the free market to flourish, driving innovation, creating wealth, and ultimately, fostering a more prosperous and free society for all.

4.1 Limited Government

A limited government, functioning as a night watchman, is the cornerstone of a thriving libertarian utopia. Its primary role isn't to dictate, but to protect. This protection manifests in upholding individual rights—the right to life, liberty, and property—the very foundations upon which free markets flourish. Think of it as the essential framework, not the driving force, of economic activity. The government's job is to ensure fair play, not to play the game itself. This means enforcing contracts impartially, maintaining a stable legal system, and ensuring the consistent application of just laws—laws that are clearly defined, easily understood, and minimally intrusive. Such a structure empowers individuals and businesses to engage in voluntary transactions without fear of arbitrary interference or coercion. It removes the uncertainty that stifles innovation and investment, allowing the market's inherent dynamism to propel progress.

The absence of excessive regulation fosters competition. Instead of creating barriers to entry and stifling entrepreneurship, a limited government allows businesses of all sizes to compete on a level playing field. This not only drives down prices for consumers, providing them with greater purchasing power and choice, but also spurs innovation. Companies are incentivized to constantly improve products and services to remain competitive, leading to a continuous cycle of enhancements and advancements. The market, not the state, determines the winners and losers, based purely on merit and consumer preference. This organic process naturally leads to efficient resource allocation, as businesses respond to fluctuating consumer demand with speed and agility impossible under heavy government control.

Furthermore, a limited government drastically reduces the burden of taxation. With fewer programs and initiatives to fund, tax rates can be significantly lower. This leaves more money in the hands of citizens and businesses, increasing their investment capacity and economic growth. Lower taxes also stimulate job creation and reduce the cost of doing business, making a nation more competitive on the global stage. Lower taxes aren't simply beneficial for the wealthy; they benefit everyone by increasing overall prosperity and allowing individuals to make their own choices about how to utilize their earnings. This system promotes personal responsibility and self-reliance, characteristics integral to a functioning libertarian society.

However, the concept of a limited government shouldn't be

misinterpreted as a complete absence of government. A minimal state still plays a crucial role in providing essential public goods that the free market struggles to deliver efficiently. National defense, for example, is a classic example; the private sector can't effectively provide national security. It's a collective good that requires centralized coordination and public funding. Similarly, the establishment and maintenance of a legal framework is vital for enforcing contracts, protecting property rights, and resolving disputes—essential functions that would otherwise be subject to chaos and inefficiency. The key lies in finding a delicate balance: enough government to provide crucial public services, but not so much that it interferes with individual liberty and the efficient operation of the free market.

Ultimately, a limited government acts as a guardian of individual liberty, not a controller of it. By fostering a fair and predictable legal environment, protecting individual rights, and providing essential public goods, it sets the stage for a dynamic, competitive, and prosperous society. It is not about reducing government involvement for its own sake, but rather to maximize individual freedom and economic growth. The optimal level of government intervention is therefore not a fixed constant but a dynamic balance achieved through careful consideration of the specific circumstances and continuous assessment of its efficacy. The emphasis remains on minimizing unnecessary interference and allowing the free market to operate according to its inherent principles. This requires constant vigilance and a commitment to the core tenets of liberty, ensuring the government's role stays focused on protection and not control.

4.2 Protecting Rights

Protecting individual rights is paramount in a truly free society. A robust legal framework, independent of undue political influence, is the cornerstone of this protection. This framework must guarantee due process, ensuring fair and impartial application of the law to all citizens. Without such a system, the very foundation of liberty crumbles under the weight of arbitrary power, leaving individuals vulnerable to the whims of those in authority. This isn't just about abstract ideals; it's about tangible security and the freedom to pursue one's life without fear of unjust persecution. The absence of such protection undermines the very essence of a free market, creating a breeding ground for corruption and hindering economic growth.

The protection of property rights is equally critical. Secure property rights incentivize investment, innovation, and economic productivity. When individuals possess confidence that their possessions – including their intellectual property and the fruits of their labor – are safe from arbitrary seizure or infringement, they are more likely to take risks, invest in the future, and contribute to overall societal prosperity. This isn't simply a matter of material wealth; it's about the protection of personal autonomy and the ability to control one's own destiny. The opposite creates a climate of uncertainty and fear, stifling economic dynamism and limiting the potential for growth. Think of it as the bedrock upon which economic advancement is built – without it, the structure inevitably fails. Freedom of contract, a cornerstone of free market operations, is indispensable. Individuals should be free to enter into agreements that benefit them, without unnecessary governmental interference. This freedom necessitates a transparent and efficient system for resolving disputes, safeguarding both parties involved. When people trust the fairness and efficiency of contract enforcement, transactions are more readily conducted, increasing the volume and depth of trade. Conversely, a system riddled with bureaucratic hurdles and corruption discourages participation, leading to inefficiency and slowing down the economic activity.

Ensuring freedom of speech and expression remains essential. Open and unfettered dialogue is the lifeblood of a vibrant society. The free exchange of ideas, even those considered controversial, is necessary for the progress of human knowledge and the refinement of our understanding of the world around us. Suppressing dissent restricts the ability to challenge existing power structures and identify potential societal problems. Furthermore, a free flow of information supports informed decision-making and fosters robust debate, leading to better-informed policies and a more responsive and adaptive society. Imagine a society where only one viewpoint is tolerated – progress would stagnate, and the potential for positive change would be stifled.

Finally, the enforcement of these rights needs to be impartial and consistent. This requires a judicial system that is independent of political influence, staffed by qualified and unbiased judges. Every individual needs equal access to justice, regardless of their social standing or economic circumstances. This crucial aspect ensures everyone has the chance to assert their rights and seek redress for any violations. An impartial judiciary acts as an effective safeguard against corruption and tyranny, ensuring the rule of law applies equally to all. A fair system bolsters public confidence in the stability and justice of the entire society, a trust that's vital for its long-term success. Without it, we're left with a system prone to abuse and lacking the key element of fairness.

5 Addressing Market Failures

Externalities represent a significant challenge to the efficient functioning of free markets. These are costs or benefits that affect parties who did not choose to incur them. Consider a factory polluting a river; downstream communities bear the environmental cost, yet they had no say in the factory's operation. This illustrates a classic negative externality. Conversely, a beekeeper's bees pollinating neighboring crops create a positive externality—the farmer benefits without directly paying for the pollination service. Addressing these requires incentivizing responsible behavior without heavy-handed government intervention. One solution is to use Pigouvian taxes, essentially taxing the negative externality to reflect its true cost. For instance, a carbon tax discourages pollution by making it more expensive, incentivizing businesses to adopt cleaner technologies. Alternatively, well-defined property rights can be crucial. Clear ownership of the river, for example, would give the downstream communities legal standing to sue the polluting factory, thereby internalizing the external cost. Market-based solutions, such as cap-and-trade systems, offer another approach, allowing businesses to buy and sell pollution permits, creating a market-driven incentive for reducing emissions. These solutions highlight how libertarian principles can be applied to resolve problems arising from externalities, aligning individual incentives with societal well-being.

The provision of public goods poses another market failure. Public goods are non-excludable and non-rivalrous; meaning that one person's consumption doesn't diminish another's, and it's difficult to prevent anyone from consuming them. National defense is a prime example. No one can be excluded from its benefits, and one person's security doesn't reduce another's. Because of these characteristics, the free market under-provides public goods, as individuals have little incentive to contribute when they can benefit without paying (the free-rider problem). However, a purely libertarian approach does offer solutions beyond simply relying on the state. Voluntary contributions, fueled by individual recognition of the public good's value, can play a significant role. Philanthropy, community initiatives, and charitable organizations demonstrate the ability of individuals to collectively fund and provide public goods in the absence of government compulsion. Furthermore, innovative market mechanisms, such as crowdfunding and subscription models, provide alternative methods for financing and allocating resources for public goods, promoting individual choice and responsibility within a framework of voluntary cooperation. These demonstrate a potential path for a free market to effectively address the provision of public goods.

Information asymmetry, where one party in a transaction possesses more information than the other, creates another market distortion. Consider the used car market: the seller typically knows more about the car's condition than the buyer. This imbalance can lead to inefficient outcomes, as buyers may be unwilling to pay a fair price, fearing hidden defects, leading to underinvestment in the market. To mitigate this, market-based mechanisms can facilitate greater transparency and accountability. Independent vehicle inspections, comprehensive warranties, and online reviews allow buyers to obtain more information, reducing the information asymmetry and promoting fairer transactions. Reputation systems, whether formal or informal, help build trust and accountability, incentivizing sellers to provide accurate information. These mechanisms don't rely on government intervention but foster voluntary information sharing and accountability, improving market efficiency within the principles of a free market. Ultimately, it's the collective pursuit of better information, driven by self-interest and market forces, that corrects for this market failure.

5.1 Externalities

Externalities represent a significant challenge to the idealized efficiency of free markets. These are costs or benefits that affect a party who did not choose to incur that cost or benefit. Think of a factory polluting a river; downstream communities suffer the consequences of water contamination, a cost they weren't party to creating. Conversely, a beautifully maintained garden might benefit neighbors, providing aesthetic pleasure they didn't pay for. Understanding externalities is crucial for navigating the complexities of a truly free market.

The core issue with externalities lies in their inherent misallocation of resources. Because the cost (or benefit) isn't directly reflected in the market price, the market price fails to accurately signal the true social cost or benefit of production or consumption. In the pollution example, the factory's production cost doesn't include the cost of cleaning up the river, leading to overproduction from a societal perspective. The market price underestimates the true cost. This leads to inefficient resource allocation – too much pollution, too little clean water. Conversely, undervalued aesthetic benefits of beautiful landscaping lead to underinvestment in beautification.

Addressing externalities without infringing upon individual liberty requires creative solutions. One approach focuses on internalizing these externalities; that is, making the producer or consumer directly accountable for the costs or benefits they create. This might involve imposing a tax on polluting activities (a "Pigovian tax"), effectively increasing the production cost to reflect the true societal cost. The revenue generated could then be used to fund environmental cleanup efforts.

Alternatively, establishing clear property rights can help alleviate the problem. If the factory's pollution directly harms a downstream landowner's property, legal recourse exists to force the factory to compensate for the damage. The court would need to assess and determine compensation, but this establishes a direct relationship between polluter and polluted. This incentivizes the factory to reduce pollution, either through technology improvements or by relocating. This framework works best with clear and easily defined property rights.

However, some externalities prove difficult to address with such direct methods. Consider the pervasive benefits of education. An educated population benefits society as a whole; however, the individual benefits of education are often insufficient to fully motivate participation. This creates a classic underinvestment in human capital, with significant societal implications. The problem's complexity stems from the diffuse nature of the benefits; tracing a direct connection between a particular individual's education and a corresponding societal benefit poses considerable challenge.

Another frequently debated example is the issue of noise pollution. While clearly a negative externality impacting nearby residents, quantifying the precise damage to create a just compensation scheme proves incredibly complex. Each individual's tolerance varies, the duration and intensity of noise differs considerably, and linking specific ailments to specific noise sources poses insurmountable difficulties. This complexity highlights the limitations of purely market-based solutions in certain situations.

While a completely unregulated free market may struggle with externalities, government intervention should be carefully considered, and its potential for unintended consequences carefully weighed. Overly burdensome regulation can stifle innovation and economic growth. The best approach lies in finding a balance between promoting a free market and addressing market failures creatively, potentially using market mechanisms to correct the imbalances. For example, tradable pollution permits—a market-based approach—offers a fascinating avenue to explore. This system lets companies buy and sell permits to pollute, creating a price for pollution which the market itself dictates, promoting efficiency in reducing it overall. Therefore, the goal isn't total elimination of government intervention, but rather the strategic and minimal use of regulation to correct market failures, respecting individual

liberty while addressing wider societal well-being.
The ideal solution is not simply to minimize government regulation as a primary goal. Rather, the goal lies in finding and implementing optimal solutions that address negative externalities through methods that align with libertarian principles. This may include the creative use of market-based incentives, the careful development of property rights, and a cautious and considered application of appropriate regulations when necessary. The key is not to abandon the free market, but to refine and enhance its capacity to allocate resources effectively even in the face of complexities posed by externalities. Striking this balance remains a continuous challenge, a delicate dance between liberty and the overall well-being of society. The challenge lies in fostering a dynamic, flexible and evolving approach to address externalities without imposing undue restrictions. Finding this equilibrium presents a critical area for continued examination and innovative solutions. The exploration of effective, freedom-respecting strategies to address externalities will remain a central point of discussion and implementation as we aim towards a truly free market future.

5.2 Public Goods

Public goods, unlike typical market commodities, present a unique challenge to the free market ideal. They are non-excludable, meaning it's difficult or impossible to prevent individuals from consuming them even if they haven't paid, and non-rivalrous, meaning one person's consumption doesn't diminish another's. National defense is a classic example; everyone benefits from a secure nation regardless of their individual contribution to its defense budget. This inherent characteristic makes it difficult for private entities to profitably provide them. The free rider problem, where individuals benefit without contributing, undermines the market mechanism. This doesn't mean, however, that a libertarian society must abandon these essential services.

A crucial aspect of navigating the public goods challenge within a libertarian framework lies in finding creative, market-based solutions. Voluntary contributions, spurred by civic duty and community spirit, represent a significant avenue. While the free rider problem remains a factor, social pressure, reputation, and a sense of shared responsibility can encourage substantial participation. Philanthropic organizations, empowered by the generosity of individuals and businesses, can play a vital role in funding and providing these services, channeling voluntary contributions into effective action. Consider the historical examples of private sector initiatives in areas like lighthouse maintenance, which were effectively managed without direct government involvement, and the countless private charities working today. These models offer valuable insights into alternative approaches.

The role of government, even within a staunchly libertarian context, needs further examination. While a minimal state is desirable, complete government abstention from public goods provision is practically infeasible. The potential for societal collapse resulting from a complete lack of national defense or disease control underscores this reality. Therefore, a carefully considered, limited government intervention might be necessary. The key lies in maintaining transparency, accountability, and minimizing the state's reach. Competitive bidding for the provision of public goods, where private entities vie for contracts, can inject market-based efficiency even within a government-supervised framework. This carefully balanced approach recognizes the free market's strengths while addressing the inherent challenges presented by public goods. Instead of direct provision, government could incentivize private sector involvement through subsidies or tax credits, fostering competition among different providers.

Furthermore, technological advancements offer promising avenues for resolving the public goods dilemma. Blockchain technology, for instance, offers innovative solutions for managing and tracking contributions, potentially mitigating the free rider problem by offering verifiable proof of participation and enhancing transparency. This transparency enables individuals to confidently contribute, knowing that their contribution will be clearly documented and effectively utilized.

Smart contracts can automate the delivery of services based on contributions, further streamlining the process. While these technologies are still evolving, their potential to revolutionize public goods provision within a decentralized, free market model is considerable. This isn't about replacing market forces, but rather harnessing technology to reinforce them.

Ultimately, a libertarian approach to public goods is not about abolishing their provision, but rather about fundamentally rethinking how they are delivered. It is about creating a system that leverages the dynamism of the free market, harnesses the power of voluntary contribution and technological innovation, and retains a limited, well-defined governmental role focusing on ensuring fairness and efficiency without unnecessarily hindering the natural forces of supply and demand. The challenge isn't to simply replace a governmental monopoly with a private one; the goal is to find a solution that is both effective and consistent with the core principles of individual liberty and limited government. This approach focuses on market mechanisms and voluntary action as much as possible, with government playing only a limited, supplementary role. It necessitates a balanced perspective, appreciating both the potential and limitations of the market in addressing the complexities of public goods provision.

5.3 Information Asymmetry

Information asymmetry, a situation where one party in a transaction possesses more information than the other, significantly undermines the efficiency of free markets. This imbalance of knowledge can lead to suboptimal outcomes, hindering the very dynamism we champion. Imagine a used car sale: the seller, often having a better understanding of the vehicle's true condition, might easily exploit this knowledge gap, potentially selling a lemon at a price reflecting a much better car. This isn't merely an isolated incident; it's a pervasive challenge that necessitates careful consideration within our pursuit of a truly free and competitive market. Transparency and access to information, therefore, become paramount.

Consumers often lack the expertise needed to fully evaluate the quality or suitability of products and services. Consider complex financial products, for instance. The average individual might struggle to comprehend the intricacies of a mortgage or investment plan, leaving them vulnerable to manipulative practices or unfavorable terms. This vulnerability is not simply a matter of individual irresponsibility; it's a systemic issue born from the inherent asymmetry of information between sophisticated providers and less informed consumers. Building a robust and ethical free market requires proactive steps to bridge this gap and empower consumers with the knowledge they need to make informed decisions.

One approach to mitigating information asymmetry involves fostering greater transparency. Mandating clear and accessible labeling, standardized product descriptions, and readily available comparative data can significantly improve consumer decision-making. Think of nutritional labels on food products, allowing consumers to make choices that better align with their health goals. Such initiatives, while possibly involving some degree of regulation, ultimately serve to strengthen the market by empowering informed choices. This is not about stifling competition but rather about establishing a level playing field where consumers aren't disadvantaged by a lack of knowledge.

Another powerful strategy is to encourage independent verification and rating systems. Consumer reviews, independent testing labs, and reputable media sources all serve as valuable tools to counter the influence of biased information. These systems, while not perfect and susceptible to manipulation, can create a powerful dynamic of transparency and accountability. The more accessible and reliable this information becomes, the less effective deceptive practices become. In short, fostering a culture that values unbiased and easily accessible information is critical in countering the effects of information asymmetry. Indeed, empowering informed consumers strengthens the very foundations of a free market.

Furthermore, investments in education and financial literacy programs can go a long way toward leveling the informational playing field. Equipping individuals with the skills to critically evaluate information, understand complex financial instruments, and navigate marketplace complexities is an investment in the future of free markets. Empowered consumers are better equipped to resist manipulation, negotiate fairer terms, and actively participate in the marketplace. This is not a passive undertaking; it necessitates a proactive approach focusing on fostering individual knowledge and capability.

Ultimately, addressing information asymmetry within a framework that respects individual liberty and minimizes government intervention requires a multi-pronged approach. It necessitates a commitment to transparency, the cultivation of independent verification systems, and a significant investment in educating consumers. The goal isn't to eliminate information asymmetry entirely—that would be an unrealistic and perhaps even undesirable aspiration—but rather to significantly reduce its negative impacts on market efficiency and consumer welfare. By empowering consumers with knowledge and tools, we can create a more robust, dynamic, and equitable free market that truly serves the interests of all participants. The path to a truly libertarian utopia rests, in part, on this crucial foundation of informed choice. Without it, the very mechanisms of a free market are compromised.

6 Social Implications

Charity and philanthropy, often seen as government responsibilities, thrive in a libertarian utopia. Individuals, empowered by their economic freedom, are more inclined to contribute voluntarily to causes they deem worthy. This fosters a diverse and responsive system of social support, catering to specific needs with greater efficiency than large-scale government programs. The decentralized nature of such giving allows for innovation and experimentation in charitable approaches, leading to potentially better outcomes for those in need. Furthermore, the absence of heavy taxation frees up more resources for individual donations, boosting the overall capacity for charitable giving. Consider the impact of removing bureaucratic hurdles and streamlining the donation process – individuals could direct their resources to the causes that resonate most strongly with their values, fostering a more compassionate and effective social safety net. The emphasis shifts from mandatory contributions to voluntary acts of generosity, creating a society where compassion is truly a choice, driven by empathy and individual responsibility rather than enforced compliance. This dynamic approach, rooted in individual freedom, creates a more nuanced and adaptable system of social support than any centrally planned alternative.

The issue of poverty and inequality requires a nuanced understanding within a libertarian framework. While disparities in wealth may exist, the focus shifts from redistributive policies to fostering opportunities for upward mobility. A free market, unburdened by excessive regulation, creates a vast array of opportunities for individuals to improve their economic standing through entrepreneurship, skill development, and hard work. Access to education and training becomes crucial, facilitating the development of a skilled workforce capable of participating fully in a dynamic economy. Rather than focusing solely on income redistribution, the emphasis is on creating an environment where everyone has a fair chance to succeed. This might involve promoting free trade and reducing barriers to entry for new businesses, empowering individuals to build their own wealth. Moreover, a robust legal framework that protects property rights and enforces contracts is fundamental. This creates a stable and predictable environment where individuals can invest in their future with confidence. A crucial element is the emphasis on individual responsibility. Empowerment through opportunity, not entitlement through

welfare, forms the bedrock of this approach. While some level of inequality is inevitable, it's essential to focus on creating a system that maximizes opportunities for all, not simply aiming for a pre-determined level of equality.
Environmental concerns are often cited as a failure of free markets. However, a well-functioning market, with appropriately defined property rights and the ability to incorporate environmental costs into market prices, can address these issues effectively. Market-based solutions like carbon taxes or cap-and-trade systems can incentivize businesses to adopt environmentally friendly practices. By placing a price on pollution, these systems create a powerful incentive for innovation and the development of cleaner technologies. A critical aspect is the proper allocation of property rights, particularly regarding natural resources. Clearly defined ownership makes individuals accountable for the environmental impact of their activities. It's crucial to avoid the pitfalls of overregulation, which can stifle innovation and economic growth. Instead, the emphasis is on fostering a system that internalizes environmental costs, allowing the market to find efficient and effective solutions. The argument against excessive regulation rests on the premise that innovation often arises from a need to adapt and improve rather than from enforced compliance. Moreover, the development of new technologies, driven by the profit motive, can create environmentally superior alter-

natives. In a truly free market, this process would naturally occur as individuals strive to make environmentally responsible choices, while the market incentivizes businesses to find more environmentally friendly ways of producing and consuming.

6.1 Charity and Philanthropy

Within a truly free market, the role of charity and philanthropy takes on a unique and vital significance. It transcends mere altruism; it becomes a fundamental component of a robust and compassionate society, a powerful force capable of addressing social needs without relying on coercive government intervention. This isn't about replacing government; it's about complementing the natural efficiency of the market with the power of voluntary giving.

The beauty of a charitable system rooted in liberty lies in its diverse and decentralized nature. Individuals and organizations, driven by their own values and priorities, freely choose to support causes they deem worthy. This contrasts sharply with government-run welfare systems, where decisions about resource allocation are often made bureaucratically and removed from the immediate needs of the individuals affected. In a libertarian utopia, donations flow directly to those in need, bypassing layers of red tape and inefficiency inherent in large-scale government programs.

Moreover, the voluntary nature of charitable giving fosters a sense of community and shared responsibility. Donors feel a direct connection to the impact of their contributions, leading to increased engagement and accountability. This active participation fosters a stronger, more resilient social fabric than one reliant solely on government mandates. We see this in countless local initiatives, community gardens, and volunteer-driven organizations that flourish organically without the heavy hand of the state.

However, some might argue that reliance on charity leaves the vulnerable unprotected and exacerbates existing inequalities. Yet, a competitive market, free of stifling regulations, creates opportunities for upward mobility. Entrepreneurial spirit blossoms, driving innovation and creating jobs, ultimately benefiting society as a whole. While some might need charitable support initially, the dynamism of a free market is better equipped to lift individuals out of poverty than any top-down approach.

Furthermore, the very act of giving freely promotes individual growth and strengthens communities. It builds empathy and understanding between donors and recipients, fostering a more harmonious society. We find that those engaged in philanthropic acts often experience a deeper sense of purpose and fulfillment, enriching their own lives in the process. This isn't merely a matter of economic efficiency; it's a question of

fostering a genuinely caring and interconnected society.
Consider the potential for technological advancements to further enhance the impact of charity. Blockchain technology, for instance, offers transparent and secure methods for tracking donations, ensuring accountability and preventing fraud. Crowdfunding platforms already demonstrate the power of harnessing collective giving for diverse projects, from disaster relief to educational initiatives. Innovation in this area has the potential to dramatically increase the effectiveness and reach of charitable endeavors.

It's crucial to acknowledge that a society relying primarily on charitable giving requires a strong legal framework upholding property rights and contracts. This ensures that donations are properly managed and that charities operate with transparency and accountability. A clear and efficient legal system doesn't stifle giving; it facilitates and protects it, preventing exploitation and ensuring that donations truly benefit their intended recipients. The system works most effectively with minimal government interference.

Ultimately, the success of a charitable system within a libertarian framework hinges on a culture of individual responsibility and generosity. It's a vision where individuals are empowered to make their own choices, freely contributing their resources to the causes they believe in. While government may have a role in ensuring a fair and just legal system for charitable giving to take place, it should refrain from direct intervention in the allocation of resources or the establishment of charitable enterprises. This ensures a dynamic and efficient approach to addressing social needs, fostering a more compassionate and prosperous society. A free market, fueled by voluntary giving, empowers individuals and communities to create a more just and equitable world.

6.2 Poverty and Inequality

Addressing poverty and inequality within a free market framework requires a nuanced approach. It's not about ignoring these issues; rather, it's about understanding how a truly competitive market, devoid of excessive government intervention, can create opportunities and foster a more equitable society than many centralized systems. The common misconception is that free markets inherently exacerbate inequality, a belief often stemming from a misunderstanding of market dynamics and the role of government in distorting them.

Many argue that a lack of government safety nets leads to widespread poverty. However, history demonstrates that heavy-handed government intervention, through welfare programs and regulations, often creates dependency and stifles individual initiative, ultimately hindering long-term economic mobility. Instead of focusing on redistribution, a free market approach prioritizes creating a level playing field where everyone has the opportunity to succeed based on their merit, skills, and ambition. This emphasis on individual responsibility is often perceived as harsh, yet it fosters self-reliance and resilience, attributes crucial for navigating economic uncertainties.

The true engine of poverty reduction lies in economic growth, and free markets are demonstrably the most effective drivers of such growth. Competition, innovation, and efficient resource allocation naturally generate wealth. While wealth distribution might appear uneven initially, a rising tide ultimately lifts all boats. A flourishing economy provides more jobs, higher wages, and expanded opportunities for individuals across all income levels, reducing poverty more effectively than any welfare program. This growth fosters a virtuous cycle; increased wealth expands the tax base, allowing for even more essential public services while minimizing the need for extensive, often ineffective, welfare programs.

While acknowledging that some level of inequality will always exist, given the inherent differences in individual skills, talents, and work ethic, the goal is not to eradicate inequality but to minimize its impact and ensure everyone has a chance to improve their circumstances. Furthermore, focusing solely on reducing income inequality can be counterproductive, as it distracts from the far more critical objective of creating widespread prosperity. A focus on reducing poverty directly, through promoting economic growth and providing access to education and job training, addresses the root cause more effectively.

Addressing poverty and inequality within a libertarian framework necessitates focusing on removing barriers to entry and promoting equal opportunity. This involves dismantling regulations that disproportionately burden small businesses and entrepreneurs, thereby limiting competition and reducing economic mobility. It also involves reforming educational systems to promote individual skills development and adaptability to the ever-evolving job market. Furthermore, a strong emphasis on property rights ensures individuals can own and control their assets, fostering a sense of ownership and incentivizing them to work towards long-term prosperity.

Charity and philanthropy play a vital role in supplementing the efforts of a free market economy. These voluntary contributions, driven by individual compassion and a sense of social responsibility, address social needs in ways that government programs often fail to do. The beauty of a free market is not merely its efficiency in generating wealth but also its ability to harness human generosity. Private charities are often more efficient and responsive to local needs, adapting to changing circumstances far more quickly than large, bureaucratic government programs. They also offer an important counterbalance to the potential drawbacks of a purely market-driven approach to social welfare, allowing for personalized support and targeted assistance.

Ultimately, the libertarian approach to poverty and inequality does not advocate for apathy or the disregard of the less fortunate. Instead, it proposes a fundamentally different approach, focusing on generating widespread economic growth and eliminating artificial barriers to upward mobility. This approach prioritizes empowering individuals to lift themselves out of poverty, through providing them with the tools and opportunities to succeed. It's not about handouts, but hand-ups; not about dependence, but empowerment. The focus is on sustainable solutions that not only alleviate poverty but also promote individual liberty and foster a dynamic, thriving society for everyone. The true measure of success, in this model, is not the absence of inequality, but the abundance of opportunity.

6.3 Environmental Concerns

Environmental protection within a free market framework might seem paradoxical at first glance. Many associate environmental degradation with unchecked industrial growth, a direct contrast to the principles of free and dynamic competition. However, a closer examination reveals that robust property rights and a clearly defined legal framework are key to environmental stewardship, rather than obstacles. A strong legal system establishing clear liability for environmental damage incentivizes businesses to adopt environmentally friendly practices, shifting away from a model that externalizes costs onto the environment and society. This isn't about government mandates; instead, it's about creating an environment where responsible behavior is rewarded and irresponsible behavior penalized.

The market can indeed provide innovative solutions. Think about the rise of green technologies. Solar power, wind energy, and energy-efficient appliances haven't become mainstream due to government subsidies alone; it's also been a result of consumer demand for cleaner and more sustainable options. Businesses responded to that demand, creating competition and driving down costs. This competitive process fosters innovation; companies constantly seek better, more efficient, and more environmentally friendly ways to produce goods and services. It's a system of checks and balances, where consumer preference dictates the direction of technological advancement. This is far more efficient and responsive to actual needs than top-down governmental mandates often are.

A system of tradable pollution permits, for example, is a powerful market-based mechanism to address pollution. This approach sets a cap on overall pollution levels, then allows companies to buy and sell permits, creating a dynamic market that incentivizes efficiency and minimizes environmental harm. Companies that can reduce emissions below their permitted levels can sell their surplus permits, generating revenue and incentivizing further environmental improvements. Those that struggle to comply would face higher costs, pushing them to innovate or improve their production process. This approach balances the need for environmental protection with the economic realities of businesses, fostering innovation and efficiency. The result is an approach that can be far more effective and far less costly than centralized government intervention.

Consider the tragedy of the commons. This economic concept illustrates how shared resources, like clean air or clean water, tend to be overexploited when there's no clear ownership or responsibility. Private property rights solve this issue. When individuals or businesses own a resource, they have a direct incentive to conserve and protect it, thereby preventing depletion. This extends to natural resources, whether it's responsible forestry management or careful water usage. The protection of these resources becomes directly linked to their economic value, encouraging proactive conservation rather than reactive governmental regulation. This translates into a more cost-effective and environmentally sound management of the resources.

Some might argue that free markets inevitably lead to environmental devastation, but this is a misconception. Free markets are merely a system of resource allocation; the values driving the market determine the outcomes. By establishing strong legal frameworks around environmental protection and promoting property rights, we can harness the power of the free market to foster environmental responsibility rather than environmental destruction. It's the role of the legal system to define and enforce environmental standards, not to dictate specific technologies or production methods. This allows for flexibility, innovation, and ultimately, greater effectiveness in achieving environmental goals.

Addressing environmental concerns is not about restricting economic activity; rather, it's about integrating environmental considerations into economic decision-making. This is achieved, not through heavy-handed governmental control, but through a framework that empowers individuals and businesses to act responsibly, recognizing that environmental protection is not only beneficial for the planet but also contributes to economic prosperity in the long run. The focus should be on aligning individual incentives with collective environmental goals, thereby leveraging the power of the free market to achieve a cleaner and more sustainable future. It's not a question of choosing between economic growth and environmental protection; it is about finding the synergistic solution that allows both to thrive.

7 The Future of Liberty

Technological advancements are rapidly reshaping our world, presenting both opportunities and challenges for the future of liberty. Consider the rise of artificial intelligence and automation; while potentially creating immense wealth and efficiency, these advancements could also exacerbate existing inequalities if not carefully managed within a framework that protects individual rights and ensures equitable access to opportunities. The key is to harness technological progress to empower individuals, not to concentrate power in the hands of a few. Regulations should focus on fostering competition and innovation, not stifling it through excessive control. A robust legal system, capable of adapting to the challenges of a technologically advanced society, will be crucial in this regard. Open-source technologies and decentralized systems could play an important role in preserving individual autonomy in the digital age, allowing individuals more control over their data and participation in the digital economy. We must ensure that these technological advancements serve to enhance individual liberty, rather than eroding it.

Global interconnectedness presents another set of complexities for the future of liberty. Globalization, while creating opportunities for trade and economic growth, also increases the potential for conflicts and the erosion of national sovereignty. A truly libertarian future requires a careful balancing act: supporting free trade and economic cooperation while safeguarding the autonomy of nations and individuals. International cooperation on issues like environmental protection and human rights is necessary but should not come at the expense of individual liberties. Ultimately, a global framework upholding principles of individual rights and free markets is vital for a future where liberty thrives across borders. International institutions should focus on resolving disputes peacefully, fostering cooperation, and promoting respect for individual rights rather than imposing centralized control or stifling innovation. A network of independent, cooperative nations, each respecting the sovereignty of others, seems an optimal structure for a world where liberty is the guiding principle.

The challenge lies in maintaining a balance between individual liberty and the collective good. While a libertarian ideal emphasizes individual autonomy, it's crucial to acknowledge the potential for negative externalities, such as environmental degradation or the spread of misinformation. Market-based solutions, such as carbon pricing or the development of robust fact-checking mechanisms, can address these concerns without sacrificing fundamental freedoms. However, we must resist the temptation to rely on overly restrictive regulations which impede innovation and hinder economic growth. Instead, we must focus on incentivizing responsible behavior and empowering individuals to make informed decisions. Transparency and accountability are vital in this regard, promoting responsible corporate behavior and mitigating the risk of exploitation. The challenge isn't to eliminate these issues, but to solve them without compromising the fundamental values of a free society.

The future of liberty also hinges on cultivating a citizenry that understands and values its freedoms. Education plays a vital role in shaping informed and engaged citizens capable of participating in a free and dynamic society. Investing in education, particularly in critical thinking and civic engagement, is essential for safeguarding individual liberties against both internal and external threats. A well-informed citizenry is better equipped to identify and resist attempts to undermine democratic institutions and limit individual freedoms. Moreover, fostering a culture of personal responsibility and civic engagement is crucial for ensuring the long-term sustainability of a libertarian society. This includes promoting voluntary participation in community initiatives and fostering a sense of shared responsibility for the common good. These are essential pillars supporting individual freedoms and ensuring a flourishing society, where both individual liberty and community thrive in synergy.

In conclusion, the future of liberty depends on our ability to adapt to rapid technological change and navigate the complexities of an increasingly interconnected world. By embracing innovation, fostering competition, and promoting a culture of personal responsibility and civic engagement, we can build a society where individual liberties are protected, and the benefits of free markets are shared by all. It requires a thoughtful balance between individual autonomy and the collective good, a continual adaptation to evolving circumstances, and a commitment to the fundamental principles of liberty, justice, and equality. This requires a constant vigilance and a proactive approach to the challenges that lie ahead. Only then can we secure a future where freedom flourishes and individuals can reach their full potential. This vision requires not only sound policy but also a shared commitment to the values of liberty and self-governance. It is a future worth striving for, a future built on the enduring principles of individual freedom and the power of free markets.

7.1 Technological Advancements

Technological advancements hold immense potential to reshape the landscape of a libertarian utopia, offering both exciting opportunities and considerable challenges. Consider, for instance, the transformative power of automation. While some fear widespread job displacement, a truly free market would allow individuals to adapt and innovate, creating new industries and opportunities previously unimaginable. The shift could lead to a surge in entrepreneurial activity, with individuals leveraging automation to pursue their passions and establish new ventures, driving economic dynamism unseen in more regulated economies. This requires a societal embrace of lifelong learning and adaptability, facilitated by a robust and flexible education system readily adjusting to emerging technological needs. Moreover, the decentralized nature of many emerging technologies, such as blockchain, aligns perfectly with libertarian principles of individual sovereignty and reduced reliance on centralized authorities.

However, this technological revolution isn't without its pitfalls. The potential for increased surveillance and data breaches necessitates a strong focus on privacy rights. A well-defined legal framework, grounded in individual liberty and property rights, is crucial to ensure that technological innovations are employed responsibly, safeguarding against potential abuses of power and protecting sensitive personal information. This means prioritizing strong encryption standards, empowering individuals with greater control over their data, and establishing clear accountability mechanisms for those who misuse technology. In the absence of robust legal safeguards, the potential benefits of technological advancement risk being overshadowed by anxieties surrounding privacy and security.

Moreover, technological progress often exacerbates existing inequalities. Access to new technologies and the skills necessary to utilize them effectively is not universally distributed. Those lacking the resources or education to participate in this technological revolution may be left behind, exacerbating societal divisions. Addressing this disparity requires a concerted effort to foster inclusive growth, ensuring everyone has the opportunity to benefit from technological advancements. This could involve initiatives that support education and training programs focused on emerging technologies, and policies that promote equitable access to technology and the information needed to use it effectively. Focusing on individual empowerment through education and skills development offers a more sustainable approach than relying on government-led redistribution efforts, which often stifle innovation and economic growth.

Another critical aspect is the ethical considerations surrounding artificial intelligence and its applications. As AI systems become more sophisticated, careful consideration must be given to the potential impact on the labor market, and the potential for algorithmic bias to perpetuate inequalities. A robust ethical framework, developed through open dialogue and informed by libertarian principles, is essential to guide the development and deployment of AI in a way that is both beneficial and just. This framework must stress transparency, accountability, and human oversight while still allowing for innovation and individual agency. Avoiding overly prescriptive regulations that stifle technological progress is paramount, while still providing necessary checks and balances to prevent misuse and maintain individual autonomy. The key lies in a balanced approach, emphasizing individual responsibility and market-based solutions to address potential ethical dilemmas.

In conclusion, the integration of technological advancements into a libertarian society presents both tremendous opportunities and significant challenges. By embracing innovation while simultaneously safeguarding individual rights, fostering equitable access to technology, and establishing robust ethical frameworks, a libertarian utopia can harness the full potential of technological progress, resulting in widespread prosperity and individual flourishing. The path forward lies not in stifling progress but in navigating the challenges proactively and strategically, ensuring that technology serves to empower individuals rather than control them, preserving and enhancing the principles of freedom and individual liberty at the heart of the envisioned society. The effective management of these complex issues will determine whether technological progress truly contributes to the realization of this utopian ideal.

7.2 Global Challenges

Globalization presents both unprecedented opportunities and significant challenges for a libertarian utopia. The free flow of goods, services, and capital, a cornerstone of free markets, is often hampered by protectionist policies enacted by national governments, hindering the efficient allocation of resources and stifling innovation. These restrictions, motivated by a desire to protect domestic industries or address perceived national security threats, ultimately harm consumers worldwide by limiting their access to a wider variety of goods and services at potentially lower prices.

However, the interconnectedness fostered by globalization also creates avenues for cooperation and the dissemination of libertarian ideals. The ease of communication and information exchange across borders facilitates the spread of free market principles and promotes the development of international networks advocating for liberty. This transnational collaboration can serve as a powerful counterbalance to nationalistic tendencies that often prioritize protectionism over free trade. Furthermore, the global nature of many modern challenges, from climate change to pandemics, necessitates collaborative solutions that transcend national boundaries.

Successfully navigating these global challenges requires a nuanced understanding of the interplay between national sovereignty and global cooperation. While individual liberty remains paramount, a purely isolationist approach is impractical and counterproductive in a globalized world. A strategy focused on fostering international cooperation while upholding individual liberties is essential. This means advocating for free trade agreements that minimize tariffs and other barriers to commerce, promoting international regulatory harmonization that avoids unnecessary red tape, and working to create international institutions that facilitate cooperation on issues that transcend national borders.

The environmental implications of global production and consumption present a particularly thorny problem for libertarians. Addressing climate change and other environmental concerns requires addressing externalities – the unintended consequences of economic activities that affect third parties. For example, the pollution generated by a factory might impose costs on neighboring communities without directly compensating them. This raises the question of how to incorporate environmental concerns within a system predicated on individual liberty and minimal government intervention. One plausible approach emphasizes market-based solutions, such as carbon taxes or cap-and-trade systems, that incentivize environmentally responsible behavior without resorting to extensive government regulation. Another method lies in promoting voluntary initiatives, whereby businesses and individuals take proactive steps to reduce their environmental footprint.

Another significant hurdle is the issue of global inequality. While free markets tend to raise overall living standards, they may not always lead to equitable distribution of wealth. The disparity between developed and developing nations creates both ethical concerns and practical challenges. Addressing this inequality requires a carefully considered approach that balances respect for national sovereignty with the need to encourage economic development in less-affluent regions. This could involve promoting foreign investment in developing countries while ensuring that such investment occurs under fair and transparent conditions, or fostering initiatives that prioritize education and technological development in underserved communities. The libertarian emphasis on individual responsibility suggests that solutions focus on empowering individuals and communities to improve their own circumstances, rather than solely relying on government redistribution programs.

Finally, the rise of new technologies presents both opportunities and risks for a libertarian society. Technological advancements can enhance productivity, improve living standards, and create new avenues for economic growth. However, they can also create new challenges relating to privacy, security, and intellectual property rights. Therefore, libertarians must advocate for policies that safeguard individual freedoms in the digital age, while ensuring that innovation is not stifled by excessive regulation or the creation of monopolies. This includes actively promoting open-source software, fostering competition in the tech sector, and prioritizing strong protection of intellectual property rights, as the market mechanisms are essential to safeguard them. Maintaining a balance between technological progress and protection of individual liberties is crucial for the continued success of a libertarian vision.

www.ingramcontent.com/pod-product-compliance
Ingram Content Group UK Ltd.
Pitfield, Milton Keynes, MK11 3LW, UK
UKHW020158290926
15471UKWH00005B/930

9 798349 388408